To

From

Date

A Special Delivery of God's
Refreshing Love

heaventy mail

words of **encouragement** *from* *God*

Philis Boultinghouse

HOWARD
PUBLISHING CO.®

Our purpose at Howard Publishing is to:

- *Increase faith* in the hearts of growing Christians
- *Inspire holiness* in the lives of believers
- *Instill hope* in the hearts of struggling people everywhere

Because He's coming again!

Heavenly Mail—Words of Encouragement from God © 2001 by Philis Boultinghouse
All rights reserved. Printed in Mexico
Published by Howard Publishing Co., Inc.
3117 North 7th Street, West Monroe, Louisiana 71291-2227

01 02 03 04 05 06 07 08 09 10   10 9 8 7 6 5 4 3 2 1

Interior design by Steve Diggs

Library of Congress Cataloging-in-Publication Data
Boultinghouse, Philis, 1951-
Heavenly mail : words of encouragement from God : a special delivery of God's
refreshing love / Philis Boultinghouse.
p. cm.
ISBN 1-58229-169-1
1. Devotional literature. I. Title.
BV4812 .B68 2001
242—dc21
00-053947

Scripture quotations are from the Holy Bible, New International Version. Copyright © 1973, 1978, 1984 by International Bible
Society. Used by permission of Zondervan Bible Publishers.

May my prayer be set before you like incense;

may the lifting up of my hands

be like the evening sacrifice.

Psalm 141:2

Contents

A Word to the Reader

Writing a letter is a special way to express yourself to someone you care for. It allows you to convey your feelings, thoughts, and emotions in a way unlike any other.

And what about receiving mail in return? Who doesn't enjoy the feeling of going to the mailbox, opening the door, and finding that you've got mail? With anticipation, you open the envelope and read the words of a cherished loved one or a faraway friend. Even though the writer is not present, you feel the warmth that the two of you share, and your hearts are united once again. That's what happens when you read *Heavenly Mail: Words of Encouragement from God.*

This unique book is filled with letters between someone like yourself and the very best friend of all—your heavenly Father. You'll quickly identify with the prayers, written as letters to a loving God, because they convey the needs, emotions, feelings, and struggles that life presents on a regular basis. In heaven's response, you'll read personalized, paraphrased scriptures, also written as letters, and you'll experience the assuring presence and loving warmth that only heaven can give.

The encouragement that fills these heavenly letters will remain with you, inspire you, and fill you with hope. Let this little book bring you closer to heaven and to words of encouragement that will impact your todays, tomorrows, and the rest of your life.

A LETTER TO *Heaven*

Dear Father,

I come to You needing Your calming peace. Lately, my heart has been all tied up in knots, and my head has been full of worry. I don't know how long it's been since I've felt truly at peace. It's as if there's a huge boulder in my life, and it's my job to carry it. I've got it up on my shoulders, but I'm crushed by its weight and I'm going nowhere.

The peace I once knew has totally left me, and it's been replaced by nagging worries and self-doubt. I've thought and thought about what I can do to fix this mess, but it seems to be out of my control. It's too big for me. I've prayed about it—oh, how I've prayed! But that big boulder is still up there.

This burden is with me in everything I do. I carry it with me everywhere I go. I can't get free of it. I long for Your peace. I ache for Your comfort. Fill me with Your peace, O Lord. Hold me in Your arms. Take this burden from me.

Your Fretful Child

A LETTER FROM *Heaven*

Dear Fretful Child,

The burden you are trying to carry is not yours—it belongs to Me. Have I not told you to cast all your anxieties on Me? If you will throw your cares on Me, I will sustain you. I never let My righteous ones fall. If you will but let Me, I will remove the burden from your shoulders and set your hands free.

Though you have prayed about your worries, you have not left them at My feet. Every time you leave My throne room, you pick them back up and take them with you. Instead of trying to figure this out on your own, you must trust in Me with all your heart. If you will acknowledge Me and My power, I will make your paths straight.

Whenever you find yourself beginning to worry, redirect your worries into fervent prayer. Pour out your heart to Me, for I am your God of refuge. Bring everything to Me— all your requests and petitions, and bring some thanks too. If you will learn to substitute prayer for anxiety, you will find that My peace will begin to fill your heart and your mind.

Whatever troubles you, you can look to Me and know that I will rescue you. I have never forsaken those who seek Me.

Your God of Rescue

*from 1 Peter 5:6–7; Psalms 55:22; 81:6–7; Proverbs 3:5–6
Psalm 62:8; Philippians 4:6–7; Psalm 9:10*

God's Word OF ENCOURAGEMENT

PSALM 55:22
Cast your cares on the LORD and he will sustain you; he will never let the righteous fall.

PSALM 62:8
Trust in him at all times, O people; pour out your hearts to him, for God is our refuge.

PSALM 81:6–7
He says, "I removed the burden from their shoulders; their hands were set free from the basket. In your distress you called and I rescued you."

1 PETER 5:6–7
Humble yourselves, therefore, under God's mighty hand, that he may lift you up in due time. Cast all your anxiety on him because he cares for you.

PHILIPPIANS 4:6–7

Do not be anxious about anything, but in everything, by prayer and petition, with thanksgiving, present your requests to God. And the peace of God, which transcends all understanding, will guard your hearts and your minds in Christ Jesus.

PROVERBS 3:5–6

Trust in the LORD with all your heart and lean not on your own understanding; in all your ways acknowledge him, and he will make your paths straight.

PSALM 9:10

Those who know your name will trust in you, for you, LORD, have never forsaken those who seek you.

A LETTER TO *Heaven*

Dear God,

Lately it seems that everything I touch turns out wrong. Every decision takes me in the wrong direction; every time I open my mouth, something stupid comes out; for every forward step I take, I take two back. I have this unsettling feeling that I've lost my way and that I just can't do anything right.

If my decisions only affected me, maybe it wouldn't be so bad; but they affect my family, my work—even my relationship with You.

I feel like such a loser.

Every morning when I get out of bed, I tell myself that today is going to be different: Today I'm going to have the right answers, make the best decisions, and handle the day's challenges with ease. But each day ends the same as the one before. I end up feeling defeated and incompetent. It's as if a black cloud is following me everywhere I go, and I can't seem to shake it no matter how hard I try.

Is there any hope for me, Lord, or am I doomed to a constant low self-esteem and feelings of failure?

Your Child Who Needs You

A Letter from *Heaven*

Dear Child,

I'm not surprised that you can't find self-confidence: You're looking in the wrong place. You're looking to yourself.

Instead of looking inward, look upward. Look to Me. I will be your confidence; I will keep you from stumbling. You concentrate on living righteously, and I'll supply you with boldness. Not only boldness, but also quietness of heart and peace.

In fact, the first step to gaining confidence and competency is recognizing that you have no competency of your own, but that all your competency comes from Me. When you place your confidence in Me, you can boldly enter My throne room in prayer, and when you ask according to My will, you can know without a doubt that I hear you. You can approach Me with freedom and confidence if you approach Me through faith in My Son.

Listen, child, I'm not finished with you yet. I have begun a good work in you, and I will carry that work to completion. You can say with confidence that I am your helper; you have no need to be afraid. You can be confident that you will see My goodness working in your life.

When you place your confidence in Me, you'll have all the confidence you need.

Your God of Confidence

from Proverbs 3:25–26; 28:1; Isaiah 32:17
2 Corinthians 3:4–5; Hebrews 4:16; 1 John 5:14
Philippians 1:6; Hebrews 13:6; Psalm 27:13

God's Word OF ENCOURAGEMENT

PROVERBS 28:1
The wicked man flees though no one pursues, but the righteous are as bold as a lion.

PROVERBS 3:25–26
Have no fear of sudden disaster or of the ruin that overtakes the wicked, for the LORD will be your confidence and will keep your foot from being snared.

HEBREWS 4:16
Let us then approach the throne of grace with confidence, so that we may receive mercy and find grace to help us in our time of need.

ISAIAH 32:17
The fruit of righteousness will be peace; the effect of righteousness will be quietness and confidence forever.

2 CORINTHIANS 3:4–5
Such confidence as this is ours through Christ before God. Not that we are competent in ourselves to claim anything for ourselves, but our competence comes from God.

1 JOHN 5:14

This is the confidence we have in approaching God: that if we ask anything according to his will, he hears us.

EPHESIANS 3:12

In him [Jesus] and through faith in him we may approach God with freedom and confidence.

PSALM 27:13

I am still confident of this: I will see the goodness of the LORD in the land of the living.

HEBREWS 13:6

So we say with confidence, "The Lord is my helper; I will not be afraid. What can man do to me?"

A Letter to *Heaven*

Dear God,

It's me—Your faraway child. A distance has been growing between us for some time now, and I'm not sure how to bridge the gap. I'm feeling disconnected from You and alone, and I want to feel the strength and comfort of Your presence. I want to run into Your powerful arms and feel the embrace of Your love wrapped firmly around me. I know in my head that You are out there and that You love me—I can almost see Your open arms extended to me in love. But even though my head knows the truth of Your love, my heart can't quite make the connection.

And what makes it even worse is that I can't figure out what's created this distance between us. Maybe it's because I haven't spent much time with You lately; I've been so preoccupied with work and my family…and with myself. Maybe it's because I've been working so hard at getting ahead in this world that I've not set my sights on Your world, on Your Son. Maybe I'm hiding some sin in my heart that I haven't quite named.

Whatever it is, Lord, I want to feel close to You; I want to find a way across this canyon between us. I want to know that I am in Your presence and that You are in mine.

Lord, pull me close to You. Clear a pathway before me that leads straight to You. I want to be with You, but I need Your help to find my way.

Your Faraway Child

A *Letter From Heaven*

Dearest Child,

It's good to hear from you. It's been quite awhile since we've talked. But I've been here all along, and I've been waiting for you. When you call upon Me and come and pray to Me, I will always listen. Of this you can be sure.

It pleases Me that you desire My presence. You may not know it, but you've already taken your first steps in your journey back to Me. Your faith that I exist and your earnest desire to seek Me will be rewarded. If you'll continue to seek Me with your heart and mind, you will find that I am not far from you at all.

Lift your eyes toward heaven and take them off the things of the world. Seek out the face of My Son. Fix your eyes on Him; look full into His face. When you do this, the path to Me will materialize before your feet.

And finally, my child, lift your heart to Me, open it, and lay it bare. Expose the sin that builds a wall between you and Me. When you acknowledge your sin, when you can face it for what it is, I will run to embrace you. I will take you into My arms and welcome you home with joy.

The gulf between us is disappearing as we speak. Welcome home.

Your Loving Father

from Hebrews 13:5; Jeremiah 29:12; Hebrews 11:6 Acts 17:27; Hebrews 12:2; Psalm 32:5; Luke 15:20–23

God's Word OF ENCOURAGEMENT

ACTS 17:27

God did this so that men would seek him and perhaps reach out for him and find him, though he is not far from each one of us.

HEBREWS 13:5

God has said, "Never will I leave you; never will I forsake you."

LUKE 15:20–23

So he got up and went to his father. But while he was still a long way off, his father saw him and was filled with compassion for him; he ran to his son, threw his arms around him and kissed him. The son said to him, "Father, I have sinned against heaven and against you. I am no longer worthy to be called your son." But the father said to his servants, "Quick! Bring the best robe and put it on him. Put a ring on his finger and sandals on his feet. Bring the fattened calf and kill it. Let's have a feast and celebrate."

JEREMIAH 29:12
Then you will call upon me and come and pray to me, and I will listen to you.

HEBREWS 12:2
Let us fix our eyes on Jesus, the author and perfecter of our faith, who for the joy set before him endured the cross, scorning its shame, and sat down at the right hand of the throne of God.

JEREMIAH 29:13–14
You will seek me and find me when you seek me with all your heart. "I will be found by you," declares the LORD.

PSALM 32:5
Then I acknowledged my sin to you and did not cover up my iniquity. I said, "I will confess my transgressions to the LORD"—and you forgave the guilt of my sin.

A LETTER TO *Heaven*

Dear God of Love,

I'm in a bit of a quandary, Lord. I've read in the Bible that you want me to love others—all others. Yet there's this one particular person—You know who I mean—whom I just can't stand to be around or even think about.

This person rubs me wrong in every way I can be rubbed. Every time I see or think about this person, my blood pressure starts to rise, I feel agitated and angry, and I start turning over in my mind all the little things about this person that bother me. My thoughts, my feelings, my emotions—even my relationship with You—have been affected.

And I hate to admit it, but part of me doesn't *want* to let go of this growing dislike. But the other part of me remembers that You love me—with all my faults, with all my shortcomings—and that You want me to love others.

The fact that your Word commands me to love others makes me think it must be something I can *choose* to do. But I'm stuck; I don't know how to will that feeling into being.

So I was thinking...since You created this world out of nothing, can You create love in me where none exists? Can you grow love in me, Lord? I want to please You, and I want my heart to be right. I need Your love in me.

Your Child Who Needs Love

A *L*ETTER FROM *Heaven*

Dear Child,

I *can* grow love in you—all I need is a willing heart. The fact that you've come to Me shows that you have such a heart. And because your heart is responsive to Me, I have heard you. You are right to note that love is a commandment. Because love is so central to who I am, it must be central to who you are as My child.

One way to grow love in your heart is to concentrate on changing your actions and your thoughts. Once you get these in line, your heart will follow. Let Me tell you how love acts and thinks: Love is patient and kind. It is protective, trusting, and hopeful. Love is not envious or boastful or proud. It is not rude or self-seeking. It is not easily angered nor does it keep a record of wrongs. Live out My definition of love. Do something *kind* for the person you dislike; check your heart to see if you are *envious* of this person; watch what you say so that it's not *rude.*

Obey Me in how you treat this person, and you will find that obedience to Me and a change of heart go hand in hand. I will give you a new heart and put a new spirit in you. I will replace your heart of stone with a heart of flesh.

You will find that as you invest yourself and your time into improving this relationship, your heart will follow your investment.

Your God of Love

from 2 Kings 22:19; John 15:12; 1 John 3:11; 4:8; 3:18
1 Corinthians 13:4–7; 1 Kings 8:61; Psalm 119:112
Deuteronomy 30:10, 6, 14; Ezekiel 36:26; Luke 12:34

God's Word OF ENCOURAGEMENT

DEUTERONOMY 30:14
The word is very near you; it is in your mouth and in your heart so you may obey it.

2 KINGS 22:19
Because your heart was responsive and you humbled yourself before the LORD...I have heard you, declares the LORD.

1 JOHN 3:11
This is the message you heard from the beginning: We should love one another.

JOHN 15:12
My command is this: Love each other as I have loved you.

1 JOHN 4:8
Whoever does not love does not know God, because God is love.

DEUTERONOMY 30:10
Obey the LORD your God and keep his commands and decrees that are written in this Book of the Law and turn to the LORD your God with all your heart and with all your soul.

1 JOHN 3:18
Dear children, let us not love with words or tongue but with actions and in truth.

1 KINGS 8:61
Your hearts must be fully committed to the LORD our God, to live by his decrees and obey his commands.

PSALM 119:112
My heart is set on keeping
your decrees to the very end.

DEUTERONOMY 30:6
The LORD your God will circumcise your hearts and the hearts of your descendants, so that you may love him with all your heart and with all your soul, and live.

LUKE 12:34
For where your treasure is,
there your heart will be also.

1 CORINTHIANS 13:4–7
Love is patient, love is kind. It does not envy, it does not boast, it is not proud. It is not rude, it is not self-seeking, it is not easily angered, it keeps no record of wrongs. Love does not delight in evil but rejoices with the truth. It always protects, always trusts, always hopes, always perseveres.

EZEKIEL 36:26
I will give you a new heart and put a new spirit in you; I will remove from you your heart of stone and give you a heart of flesh.

A Letter to *Heaven*

Dear God in Heaven,

I'm crying out to You, God, but I don't even know if You're listening. I certainly don't deserve to have You listen to me. I've failed You so many times.

I know Your Word says that You are a God of love, but I have a hard time believing that Your love could reach all the way down to me. I've made too many mistakes, blown it too many times. I don't see how a perfect God like You could love a wreck like me.

I try, Lord, I really do. But at the end of every day, I look back and all I can see is failure —failure in relationships, failure in my work…and most definitely failure at pleasing You. Others around me seem to have it so together. I see their smiles, I hear their laughter, and I hear them talk about their successes. When I compare my life to theirs, it's just one big zero.

I know I'm not worthy of Your time—much less Your love. But God, something in me won't let go of the hope that maybe You do love me—not for anything good in me—but just because that's the kind of God You are. Is that possible, God? Is there a chance for me? Do You hear my prayer? Do You care about me? Do You even know my name?

Hoping You Are There

A *Letter From Heaven*

Dear Beloved,

My heart is filled with compassion for your pain and fears. I hear you, child. I hear you, and I love you with an everlasting love. My love for you is as high as the heavens are above the earth. I have removed your failures and your sins as far from you as the east is from the west.

You need to understand that My love for you has nothing to do with who you are and that it has everything to do with who I am. You are right to see yourself as unworthy. I do not treat you as you deserve or repay you according to your successes or failures. Yes, on your own you are unworthy, but when you come to Me in faith and repentance, you are clothed with the righteousness of Christ. Your worth comes not from what you do but from your faith in My Son.

You ask if I know your name: Child, not only do I know your name; I know everything about you. I know when you get up in the morning and when you sit down to rest. I know what you are about to say before you say it. I even knew you in your mother's womb before you were ever born.

You are worth everything to Me, My child. And to prove it, I gave the life of My Son so that one day we can be together forever.

Your Faithful God of Love

from Jeremiah 31:3; Psalm 103:11–14; Lamentations 3:22–23; Psalms 4:3; 100:5; 106:1; Deuteronomy 7:7–8 Psalm 103:10; Galatians 3:27; Philippians 3:9 Psalm 139:1–4, 13–16; Romans 8:32

God's Word OF ENCOURAGEMENT

JEREMIAH 31:3
The LORD appeared to us in the past, saying: "I have loved you with an everlasting love; I have drawn you with loving-kindness."

PSALM 4:3
Know that the LORD has set apart the godly for himself; the LORD will hear when I call to him.

PSALM 100:5
For the LORD is good and his love endures for ever; his faithfulness continues through all generations.

PSALM 106:1
Praise the LORD. Give thanks to the LORD, for he is good; his love endures for ever.

PSALM 139:13–16
For you created my inmost being; you knit me together in my mother's womb. I praise you because I am fearfully and wonderfully made; your works are wonderful, I know that full well. My frame was not hidden from you when I was made in the secret place. When I was woven together in the depths of the earth, your eyes saw my unformed body. All the days ordained for me were written in your book before one of them came to be.

PHILIPPIANS 3:9
[I will] be found in him, not having a righteousness of my own that comes from the law, but that which is through faith in Christ—the righteousness that comes from God and is by faith.

GALATIANS 3:27
All of you who were baptized into Christ have clothed yourselves with Christ.

DEUTERONOMY 7:7–8
The LORD did not set his affection on you and choose you because you were more numerous than other peoples, for you were the fewest of all peoples. But it was because the LORD loved you and kept the oath he swore to your forefathers that he brought you out with a mighty hand and redeemed you from the land of slavery, from the power of Pharaoh king of Egypt.

PSALM 103:10
He does not treat us as our sins deserve or repay us according to our iniquities.

PSALM 103:11–14
For as high as the heavens are above the earth, so great is his love for those who fear him; as far as the east is from the west, so far has he removed our transgressions from us. As a father has compassion on his children, so the LORD has compassion on those who fear him; for he knows how we are formed, he remembers that we are dust.

PSALM 139:1–4
LORD, you have searched me and you know me. You know when I sit and when I rise; you perceive my thoughts from afar. You discern my going out and my lying down; you are familiar with all my ways. Before a word is on my tongue you know it completely, O LORD.

A LETTER TO *Heaven*

Dear Lord,

For a long time, now, I've told myself "that's just the way I am." Some people are timid and shy; some are outgoing and expressive; I'm just up-front and honest about my feelings— if something makes me mad, I don't hold it in. I tell people exactly what I think and how I feel. If they don't like it, that's tough—it's just the way I am.

But lately, Your Spirit has been convicting me, Lord, and I'm beginning to see that You want me to be more than "the way I am." I'm beginning to see that You continually call me higher—to be more than who I am naturally.

But knowing that I need to control my temper is not the same thing as doing it. Each day I wake up determined to do better, but by the end of the day I've blown it by blowing up. I can see, now, how my words and harshness hurt people, but I just don't know if I'm going to be able to change. Each failure brings another dose of discouragement. Is there any hope for change in me?

Can You help me, Lord?

Your Hot-Tempered Child

A LETTER FROM *Heaven*

Dear Beloved,

There is hope for you to change! The very same power that I exerted to raise My Son from the dead is available for all who believe. It is available to you.

When people do things that irritate you—and there is no doubt that they will—don't respond out of anger or in haste. Hold your tongue and take some time to think. The more you say when you're angry, the more likely you are to say something you shouldn't. And when you can go beyond merely holding your tongue and actually choose to overlook the offense, you show your wisdom by your patience. If you can learn to put your own feelings aside and consider what is best for the other person, you will be one step closer to being like My Son.

So keep close watch of your words and keep your anger under control. If you can keep your cool in the heat of an argument, you will find that a quiet word from you will often calm the anger of others as well as your own.

Keep this guideline close to your heart at all times: Be quick to listen, slow to speak, and slow to become angry.

You can change. That's what following My Son is all about. I'm in the business of making old things new.

Your Dynamic God of Change

from Ephesians 1:18–20; Romans 3:23
Proverbs 29:11; 10:19; 19:11; Philippians 2:3–4
Proverbs 16:23; 15:1; James 1:19; 2 Corinthians 5:17

God's Word OF ENCOURAGEMENT

PROVERBS 29:11
A fool gives full vent to his anger, but a wise man keeps himself under control.

EPHESIANS 1:18–20
I pray also that the eyes of your heart may be enlightened in order that you may know the hope to which he has called you, the riches of his glorious inheritance in the saints, and his incomparably great power for us who believe. That power is like the working of his mighty strength, which he exerted in Christ when he raised him from the dead and seated him at his right hand in the heavenly realms.

PROVERBS 19:11
A man's wisdom gives him patience; it is to his glory to overlook an offense.

ROMANS 3:23
For all have sinned and fall short of the glory of God.

2 CORINTHIANS 5:17
Therefore, if anyone is in Christ, he is a new creation; the old has gone, the new has come!

PHILIPPIANS 2:4
Each of you should look not only to your own interests, but also to the interests of others.

PROVERBS 15:1
A gentle answer turns away wrath, but a harsh word stirs up anger.

JAMES 1:19
My dear brothers, take note of this: Everyone should be quick to listen, slow to speak and slow to become angry.

PROVERBS 16:23
A wise man's heart guides his mouth, and his lips promote instruction.

A LETTER TO *Heaven*

Dear Lord,

I come to You, today, embarrassed at my weakness and troubled by my lack of faith. I believe in You, Lord—I really do—but sometimes my shield of faith falls and I am blind-sided by Satan's flaming arrows of doubt. I remind myself of the father who asked Jesus to heal his son: "I believe, help my unbelief."

I struggle when things don't turn out like I had expected—especially when I've prayed about them. I struggle when someone I love is hurting and no relief is in sight. I struggle when someone I love is hurting me. I struggle when my personal growth is slow, when the things that have plagued me for years still trip me up.

When I'm bombarded with difficulties—in relationships, at work, with finances, with health problems—I hate to admit it, Father, but my faith wavers and in my self-pity, I doubt Your love. Especially when the really big hurts come—like when someone I love and need dies…or leaves. In times like those, I sometimes wonder if You're even there.

Right now, Lord, I need to hear Your words of encouragement; I need to know that You are near, that Your power is at work in my life. I need to know that You see the doubt in my heart yet still love me and won't reject me. As Jesus answered the doubting father, I hear Jesus' words in my heart: "*If* I can. Anything is possible to those who believe." I believe, Lord, help my unbelief.

Your Doubting Child

A LETTER FROM *Heaven*

Dear Doubting Child,

Your quest for increased faith pleases Me. Be encouraged to know that I will reward you for your efforts to seek Me.

The first thing you need to understand as you seek to grow in faith is that faith does not begin in you. The source of faith is My own Son. He is the author and perfecter of your faith. As you fix your eyes on Him, your faith will grow.

It will also help you to remember past times that I have helped you. Think on the ways I've helped others you know; look in My Word to be reminded that I've always taken care of those who follow Me.

It's true that life in this world is difficult at times and that things don't always turn out as you desire. But know this: I take all the events of your life—the good and the bad—and I weave them together for your ultimate good. And find comfort in knowing that the tough times you go through actually serve to polish and refine you until you have the purity and the shine of the finest gold.

No matter what happens in this life, remember that I am a God of power. Nothing is impossible with Me. I am also a God of hope, and I will fill you with all joy and peace as you trust in Me. Trust in Me with all your heart; acknowledge Me in all you do, and I will make all your paths straight.

Your Faithful God

*from Hebrews 11:6; 12:2; Deuteronomy 32:7
Psalm 105:5; 1 Peter 1:6–7; Luke 1:37
Romans 15:13; Proverbs 3:5–6*

God's Word OF ENCOURAGEMENT

HEBREWS 11:6
Without faith it is impossible to please God, because anyone who comes to him must believe that he exists and that he rewards those who earnestly seek him.

HEBREWS 12:2
Let us fix our eyes on Jesus, the author and perfecter of our faith.

PSALM 105:5
Remember the wonders he has done, his miracles, and the judgments he pronounced.

DEUTERONOMY 32:7
Remember the days of old; consider the generations long past. Ask your father and he will tell you, your elders, and they will explain to you.

LUKE 1:37
Nothing is impossible with God.

1 PETER 1:6–7
In this you greatly rejoice, though now for a little while you may have had to suffer grief in all kinds of trials. These have come so that your faith—of greater worth than gold, which perishes even though refined by fire—may be proved genuine and may result in praise, glory and honor when Jesus Christ is revealed.

ROMANS 15:13
May the God of hope fill you with all joy and peace as you trust in him, so that you may overflow with hope by the power of the Holy Spirit.

A LETTER TO *Heaven*

Dear God,

I don't know any other way to tell You than to just come out and say it: I've let You down, Father, and I am so sorry.

It happened the same way it's happened so many times before: I felt the pull of the temptation. I walked over to take a closer look—telling myself that I wouldn't get too close. But I just keep walking—closer and closer. With each step my conscious thoughts—of You, of what I was about to do, of where I was going—began to shut down.

By the time I got to the edge of it, I was numb. Numb to You. Numb to the promises I've made. Numb to the hurt my actions would cause me and those I love. All the warnings I'd heard just a short while before were silenced. My mind and my heart were iced over with nothingness. And then I took the final step. It was as if I were on autopilot.

Then when the deed was done, the freeze on my heart began to thaw and reality began to dawn once again. The ache in my heart began anew. The shame. The regret.

It took everything in me to come to You this time. Voices in my head tried to tell me that You were sick of my weakness. Sick of my sin. Sick of me. But somewhere deep in my heart, I remembered Your Son and His sacrifice.

Lord God, is it possible for me to finally master this sin? Will I ever have victory over it? Do You even hear me after I've disappointed You so many times?

Your Penitent Child

A LETTER FROM *Heaven*

My Dear Child,

When you disobey Me, it breaks My heart. I've loved you and called you; I've taken you by the arms, and I've healed you. I've led you with cords of kindness and with ties of love. Yet at times, the more I call you, the farther you go from Me.

But child, I see that *your* heart is broken too. And though I live in a high and holy place, I also live with those who are contrite and lowly in spirit. With Me you will find unfailing love and full redemption.

You can overcome your sinful desire, but you must stay away from those tempting situations and walk only in the light. It is in the light that you will find fellowship with other Christians and where you will find the blood of My Son, who purifies you from your sin. Choose your friends carefully, for bad company corrupts good character.

Gain control of yourself and stay on the alert. For your enemy, the devil, prowls around like a roaring lion, looking for someone to devour. But you must resist him and stand firm in your faith. If you don't do what is right, he is crouching at your door, ready to pounce on you; he desires to have control of you. But you must master him. And with My help and the help of My Son, you can! For the one who is in you is greater than the one who is in the world.

Your Compassionate Father

from Hosea 11:1–4; Isaiah 57:15; Psalm 130:7
1 John 1:7; 1 Corinthians 15:33; 1 Peter 5:8–9
Genesis 4:7; 1 John 4:4

God's Word OF ENCOURAGEMENT

HOSEA 11:1–4
When Israel was a child, I loved him, and out of Egypt I called my son. But the more I called Israel, the further they went from me. It was I who taught Ephraim to walk, taking them by the arms; but they did not realize it was I who healed them. I led them with cords of human kindness, with ties of love; I lifted the yoke from their neck and bent down to feed them.

1 CORINTHIANS 15:33
Do not be misled: "Bad company corrupts good character."

1 JOHN 1:7
But if we walk in the light, as he is in the light, we have fellowship with one another, and the blood of Jesus, his Son, purifies us from all sin.

ISAIAH 57:15
For this is what the high and lofty One says—he who lives forever, whose name is holy: "I live in a high and holy place, but also with him who is contrite and lowly in spirit, to revive the spirit of the lowly and to revive the heart of the contrite."

1 PETER 5:8–9
Be self-controlled and alert. Your enemy the devil prowls around like a roaring lion looking for someone to devour. Resist him, standing firm in the faith.

1 JOHN 4:4
You, dear children, are from God and have overcome them, because the one who is in you is greater than the one who is in the world.

PSALM 130:7
O Israel, put your hope in the LORD, for with the LORD is unfailing love and with him is full redemption.

GENESIS 4:7
If you do what is right, will you not be accepted? But if you do not do what is right, sin is crouching at your door; it desires to have you, but you must master it.

A *Letter* to *Heaven*

Dear Heavenly Father,

I come to You, Lord, hoping You can help me overcome a growing problem. Lately, I've felt a growing presence in my life—a menacing presence, an overwhelming uneasiness. And I've finally figured out what it is. It's fear. I don't really know when it started or why, but it's getting stronger, and I'm getting weaker. It has knocked me to my knees.

And that's where I am now, Father—on my knees before You.

I've been trying to figure out what I'm afraid of. It's a lot of things. I'm afraid of not measuring up, afraid of making mistakes, afraid of what the future holds, afraid of letting my loved ones down—afraid of letting You down.

Father, I know You've called me to trust You and that You've commissioned me to live boldly. I want to be brave; I want to live fearlessly—but I need Your help. Lord, instill me with Your courage, for I have none of my own. Fill me with Your fortitude, for I am so very weak. Infuse me with the conviction that I can do all things with Your help. Train my heart to be brave.

Please take the fear from my heart and replace it with confidence and courage to live the life You have called me to.

Fearfully Yours

A LETTER FROM *Heaven*

Dearest Child of Mine,

Come to Me, My child, for I desire to gather you in My arms and carry you close to My heart.

The world you live in is a frightening place—for you live in a fallen world and it is under the control of the Evil One—but fear has no place in the hearts of My children. Fear is from the Evil One, and he uses it to cloud your view of My face. The only way to combat your fear is by trusting Me.

I have not given you a spirit of timidity and fear. Rather, I have given you a spirit of power and love and self-discipline. Always remember that because you are My child, you have already overcome the forces of this world; for I am in you, and I am greater than the prince of this world.

As long as I am beside you, you have no reason to fear, for I will help you. And I vow to you, on the life of My own Son, that I will never forsake you and that I will never leave you.

This is My charge: Stand firm in your faith in Me. Do not be afraid or discouraged. And when fear grips your heart, fix your eyes on My Son and continue to live the life that I have set before you. Do not be distracted by the battle around you; for the battle is not yours, but Mine, and I will fight it for you.

Your God of Strength

from Isaiah 40:11; 1 John 5:19; John 14:1; 2 Timothy 1:7
1 John 5:4; 4:4; Romans 8:32; Deuteronomy 31:8
1 Corinthians 16:13; Hebrews 12:1–2; 2 Chronicles 20:15

God's Word OF ENCOURAGEMENT

DEUTERONOMY 31:8

The LORD himself goes before you and will be with you; he will never leave you nor forsake you. Do not be afraid; do not be discouraged.

ISAIAH 40:11

He tends his flock like a shepherd: He gathers the lambs in his arms and carries them close to his heart; he gently leads those that have young.

2 TIMOTHY 1:7

For God did not give us a spirit of timidity, but a spirit of power, of love and of self-discipline.

HEBREWS 12:1–2

Therefore, since we are surrounded by such a great cloud of witnesses, let us throw off everything that hinders and the sin that so easily entangles, and let us run with perseverance the race marked out for us. Let us fix our eyes on Jesus, the author and perfecter of our faith, who for the joy set before him endured the cross, scorning its shame, and sat down at the right hand of the throne of God.

1 JOHN 5:4

Everyone born of God over-comes the world. This is the victory that has overcome the world, even our faith.

1 CORINTHIANS 16:13

Be on your guard; stand firm in the faith; be men of courage; be strong.

1 JOHN 5:19

We know that we are children of God.

ROMANS 8:32

He who did not spare his own Son, but gave him up for us all—how will he not also, along with him, graciously give us all things?

2 CHRONICLES 20:15

He said: "Listen, King Jehoshaphat and all who live in Judah and Jerusalem! This is what the LORD says to you: 'Do not be afraid or discouraged because of this vast army. For the battle is not yours, but God's.'"

A *L*ETTER TO *Heaven*

Dear God in Heaven,

I come to You with my heart in my hands. My heart's desire, Father, is to please You—to live a life You can be proud of. Your Word speaks of living a life worthy of my calling, and that is what I want to do.

Yet I fail You every single day, and I am so far from who You want me to be. I am easily distracted by the petty things of this world, and it doesn't take much to pull my focus from You and onto the problems in my life.

But, Father, I'm willing to be shaped and molded by You. I want to be a source of blessing and encouragement to others. I want to be an instrument in Your mighty hands. I want to be Your hands, Your feet, and Your arms in this world.

But I am so weak, and I've failed so many times. Is my life one that You can use? I want to be worthy of Your call.

Your Willing but Weak Servant

A LETTER FROM *Heaven*

Dear Servant Child,

You can be completely confident, My child, that the good work I began in you will be carried to completion. For I am continually at work in you to bring about My good purpose. Just as a potter gives shape to clay on the potter's wheel, so will I shape you to bring about My will.

The weakness you see in yourself actually works to My advantage, for My power is most effective in your weakness. In fact, the very power of Christ rests on you when you are weak. I have chosen to use what this world sees as foolishness and weakness to shame the "wise" and the "strong."

You can be assured that I, the God who brought Jesus back from the dead, will equip you with everything you need for doing My will. You are My workmanship—created for the very purpose of doing good works. In fact, I prepared good things for you to do before you were even born. And now I will empower you to fulfill your good intentions and to live out your actions prompted by faith.

I have placed special gifts within you. I encourage you not to neglect them but to fan them into flame. Use the gifts I have given you to administer My grace in its many forms.

My Word instructs you how to live to please Me—and this you are doing. I urge you to do it more and more.

Your Equipping Father

from Philippians 1:6; 2:13; Jeremiah 18:6; Isaiah 64:8
2 Corinthians 12:9–10; 1 Corinthians 1:27
Hebrews 13:20–21; Ephesians 2:10; 2 Thessalonians 1:11–12
1 Timothy 4:14; 1:6; 1 Peter 4:10; 1 Thessalonians 4:1

God's Word OF ENCOURAGEMENT

PHILIPPIANS 2:13

It is God who works in you to will and to act according to his good purpose.

JEREMIAH 18:6

"O house of Israel, can I not do with you as this potter does?" declares the LORD. "Like clay in the hand of the potter, so are you in my hand, O house of Israel."

ISAIAH 64:8

Yet, O LORD, you are our Father. We are the clay, you are the potter; we are all the work of your hand.

1 CORINTHIANS 1:27

But God chose the foolish things of the world to shame the wise; God chose the weak things of the world to shame the strong.

HEBREWS 13:20–21

May the God of peace, who through the blood of the eternal covenant brought back from the dead our Lord Jesus, that great Shepherd of the sheep, equip you with everything good for doing his will, and may he work in us what is pleasing to him, through Jesus Christ, to whom be glory for ever and ever.

1 THESSALONIANS 4:1

Finally, brothers, we instructed you how to live in order to please God, as in fact you are living. Now we ask you and urge you in the Lord Jesus to do this more and more.

EPHESIANS 2:10

For we are God's workmanship, created in Christ Jesus to do good works, which God prepared in advance for us to do.

2 TIMOTHY 1:6

I remind you to fan into flame the gift of God, which is in you through the laying on of my hands.

2 THESSALONIANS 1:11–12

With this in mind, we constantly pray for you, that our God may count you worthy of his calling, and that by his power he may fulfill every good purpose of yours and every act prompted by your faith. We pray this so that the name of our Lord Jesus may be glorified in you, and you in him, according to the grace of our God and the Lord Jesus Christ.

1 PETER 4:10

Each one should use whatever gift he has received to serve others, faithfully administering God's grace in its various forms.

1 TIMOTHY 4:14

Do not neglect your gift, which was given you through a prophetic message when the body of elders laid their hands on you.

A LETTER TO *Heaven*

Dear God!

Help me, Father, I'm sinking. I'm almost under. I feel powerless to fight the forces that are pulling me down. And I'm sorry to say that part of me doesn't want to fight. I know that what I'm pursuing is wrong, but I can't seem to stop. I can't get out of this quicksand.

My desire for this thing—this thing that my heart is pursuing—is powerful, Lord. And in my rational moments, like this one, I know it is not what You want for me—but I can't seem to pull myself away.

Yet Father, I am troubled by my sin, and I really do want to do right. And when I don't want to do right, there's still a part of me that wants to want to please You. Please hear this weak cry of my heart. My throat is parched, and my tongue sticks to the roof of my mouth when I try to call Your name.

Hear my cry. I'm sinking, Lord. Please save me.

Your Desperate Child

A *L*ETTER FROM *Heaven*

Dear Beloved,

I hear you, My child. I see your struggle. Though you may feel alone and unheard, let Me assure you that I have heard your cry and that I am very near.

It will help you to know that the struggle you face has been faced by many others. You are not alone. And you can also be assured that I have provided a way out.

This is what you must do: Humble yourself before Me, submit your heart to Me, and move closer to Me. Grieve your sin and change your laughter to mourning and your joy to gloom. When you bow down before Me and admit your dependence on Me, I will lift you up. I will rescue you from the darkness, for I have purchased your freedom with the blood of My Son.

You are My beloved child, and I will fight this battle for you. Take your stand against the devil and watch Me do the fighting. Resist him, and he will lose his power and run away.

Remember that I am in you and that I am stronger than the Evil One of the world. Because this is true, you can overcome this struggle. You can be victorious. In fact, I have already given you victory through My Son and your Lord—Jesus Christ.

You were right to come to Me. I do not despise your need for help. My arms are open wide. I'm ready to catch you. Fall on Me.

Your Loving Father

from Isaiah 41:10; 1 Corinthians 10:13; James 4:7–10
Colossians 1:13-14; 1 Samuel 17:47; 2 Chronicles 20:15
1 Corinthians 15:57; Psalms 69:33; 102:17

God's Word OF ENCOURAGEMENT

1 SAMUEL 17:47
All those gathered here will know that it is not by sword or spear that the LORD saves; for the battle is the LORD's, and he will give all of you into our hands.

1 CORINTHIANS 10:13
No temptation has seized you except what is common to man. And God is faithful; he will not let you be tempted beyond what you can bear. But when you are tempted, he will also provide a way out so that you can stand up under it.

1 CORINTHIANS 15:57
But thanks be to God! He gives us the victory through our Lord Jesus Christ.

COLOSSIANS 1:13–14
For he has rescued us from the dominion of darkness and brought us into the kingdom of the Son he loves, in whom we have redemption, the forgiveness of sins.

PSALM 69:33

The LORD hears the needy and does not despise his captive people.

PSALM 102:17

He will respond to the prayer of the destitute; he will not despise their plea.

JAMES 4:7–10

Submit yourselves, then, to God. Resist the devil, and he will flee from you. Come near to God and he will come near to you. Wash your hands, you sinners, and purify your hearts, you double-minded. Grieve, mourn and wail. Change your laughter to mourning and your joy to gloom. Humble yourselves before the Lord, and he will lift you up.

2 CHRONICLES 20:15

Do not be afraid or discouraged because of this vast army. For the battle is not yours, but God's.

A LETTER TO *Heaven*

Dear God,

I don't mean to sound ungrateful, but how long must I wait before You answer my prayer? I've come to You over and over on this matter, but nothing seems to change. I see others around me having their requests answered, yet here I sit in the same predicament.

Have I done something to offend You? Are You ignoring me to punish me? It feels as if You are hiding Your face from me or as if my prayers reach the ceiling of my house and go no farther. Every day, thoughts of defeat plague me, and my heart is full of sorrow. I know that You have the power to act on my behalf. I don't understand why You're taking so long.

I need to know that You hear me. I need to know that You care. Are You listening?

Waiting on You

A LETTER FROM *Heaven*

Dear Child,

Let Me assure you, My weary child, that My eyes are upon you and that My ears are attentive to your prayer. I exhort you to be brave and courageous as You wait on Me, for I will never forsake you. Even if you don't understand My timing or My answer to your prayer, know with full assurance that all My ways are perfect and just. I am good to those who continually seek Me and whose hope is in Me. It is good to wait quietly for My salvation.

No matter what you are going through right now, nothing can separate you from My love. If you will maintain your hope in Me, I will renew your strength. You will soar on wings like eagles; you will run and not grow weary; you will walk and not faint.

Take heart and be strong and wait on Me. Wait for Me as a watchman waits for the light of dawn. Be assured that I long to be gracious to you; that I get off My throne and on My feet to show compassion to you. You are blessed if you wait on Me. There never has been nor will there ever be a God besides Me who acts on behalf of those who wait on Him. Watch in hope for My hand to move on your behalf; wait for Me and know that I hear you.

While you wait, be encouraged by the assurance of My love.

Worth the Wait

from 1 Peter 3:12; Deuteronomy 31:6; 32:4
Lamentations 3:24–26; Romans 8:38–39; Isaiah 40:31
Psalms 27:14; 130:6; Isaiah 30:18; 64:4; Micah 7:7; Jude 21

God's Word OF ENCOURAGEMENT

ROMANS 8:38–39
For I am convinced that neither death nor life, neither angels nor demons, neither the present nor the future, nor any powers, neither height nor depth, nor anything else in all creation, will be able to separate us from the love of God that is in Christ Jesus our Lord.

DEUTERONOMY 31:6
Be strong and courageous. Do not be afraid or terrified because of them, for the LORD your God goes with you; he will never leave you nor forsake you.

1 PETER 3:12
For the eyes of the Lord are on the righteous and his ears are attentive to their prayer, but the face of the Lord is against those who do evil.

DEUTERONOMY 32:4
He is the Rock, his works are perfect, and all his ways are just. A faithful God who does no wrong, upright and just is he.

LAMENTATIONS 3:24–26
I say to myself, "The LORD is my portion; therefore I will wait for him." The LORD is good to those whose hope is in him, to the one who seeks him; it is good to wait quietly for the salvation of the LORD.

ISAIAH 40:31

Those who hope in the LORD will renew their strength. They will soar on wings like eagles; they will run and not grow weary, they will walk and not be faint.

JUDE 21

Keep yourselves in God's love as you wait for the mercy of our Lord Jesus Christ to bring you to eternal life.

PSALM 27:14

Wait for the LORD; be strong and take heart and wait for the LORD.

PSALM 130:6

My soul waits for the Lord more than watchmen wait for the morning, more than watchmen wait for the morning.

MICAH 7:7

But as for me, I watch in hope for the LORD, I wait for God my Savior; my God will hear me.

ISAIAH 64:4

Since ancient times no one has heard, no ear has perceived, no eye has seen any God besides you, who acts on behalf of those who wait for him.

ISAIAH 30:18

The LORD longs to be gracious to you; he rises to show you compassion. For the LORD is a God of justice. Blessed are all who wait for him!

A Letter to *Heaven*

Dear Lord of Heaven,

I'm coming to You with a hunger in my heart and a longing in my soul. What I'm wanting is more of You in me.

You are so high above me, so lofty and majestic. Is it possible that I, a human, could have a real relationship with You? I go to church, I pray, I try to live right and be kind; but it's You I'm wanting more of. I want to be aware of Your presence throughout my day. I want to be guided by Your hand continually.

During the fleeting moments when I am aware of Your presence in me, I'm filled with such a sense of peace and purpose. I want more of this. I want to go deeper into You.

I want the essence of me to be You. I want to be defined by You, and I want that definition to define who I am to others. Fill me with Your presence, Lord—so full that there's no room for me. And as I become filled with You, let me overflow in actions of kindness, wisdom, unselfishness, and love to others.

Is what I desire even possible? Do You desire this intimacy with me?

Wanting You

A *L*ETTER FROM *Heaven*

Dear Seeking Child,

I *will* be found by you! I never forsake those who seek Me. In fact, I am continually on the lookout for those who are looking for Me. When you seek Me with all your heart, I assure you that you will find Me. As you come near to Me, I will respond by coming near to you. I am near to all who call Me. I am near to you.

If you truly desire intimacy with Me, you will find it as you humble yourself, pray, and seek My face. As a child reaches out to her mother's face and pulls it to her own, you must seek to gaze into My eyes, into My heart; you must come to Me face to face.

My heart yearns for relationship with you as a father yearns for relationship with his child. And like a mother hen desires to gather her chicks under her wing, I desire to gather you to Me. I delight in you and have great compassion for you.

The way to lose yourself in Me is to die to yourself—just as Christ died for you—then My Son will live in you and you will be filled with Him. As Christ dwells in your heart by faith, My fullness will live in you also. And the fuller you are of Me, the more My goodness with spill over into the lives of others as you exercise the gifts I have given you.

Your God of Love

from Psalms 9:10; 14:2; Jeremiah 29:13–14; James 4:8
Psalm 145:18; 2 Chronicles 7:14; 1 Chronicles 16:10–11
Matthew 23:37; Jeremiah 31:20; Galatians 2:20
Colossians 2:9–10; Ephesians 3:16–19; 4:11–13

God's Word OF ENCOURAGEMENT

PSALM 14:2
The LORD looks down from heaven on the sons of men to see if there are any who understand, any who seek God.

1 CHRONICLES 16:10–11
Glory in his holy name; let the hearts of those who seek the LORD rejoice. Look to the LORD and his strength; seek his face always.

JEREMIAH 31:20
"Is not Ephraim my dear son, the child in whom I delight? Though I often speak against him, I still remember him. Therefore my heart yearns for him; I have great compassion for him," declares the LORD.

MATTHEW 23:37
O Jerusalem, Jerusalem, you who kill the prophets and stone those sent to you, how often I have longed to gather your children together, as a hen gathers her chicks under her wings, but you were not willing.

GALATIANS 2:20

I have been crucified with Christ and I no longer live, but Christ lives in me. The life I live in the body, I live by faith in the Son of God, who loved me and gave himself for me.

EPHESIANS 4:11–13

It was he who gave some to be apostles, some to be prophets, some to be evangelists, and some to be pastors and teachers, to prepare God's people for works of service, so that the body of Christ may be built up until we all reach unity in the faith and in the knowledge of the Son of God and become mature, attaining to the whole measure of the fullness of Christ.

EPHESIANS 3:16–19

I pray that out of his glorious riches he may strengthen you with power through his Spirit in your inner being, so that Christ may dwell in your hearts through faith. And I pray that you, being rooted and established in love, may have power, together with all the saints, to grasp how wide and long and high and deep is the love of Christ, and to know this love that surpasses knowledge—that you may be filled to the measure of all the fullness of God.

COLOSSIANS 2:9–10

For in Christ all the fullness of the Deity lives in bodily form, and you have been given fullness in Christ, who is the head over every power and authority.

A LETTER TO *Heaven*

Dear God of Deliverance,

My life, my world has come to a sudden halt. All that I know, all that makes me feel safe has been suddenly stripped from me. I've lost my bearings—I don't know which way is up and which way is down. My hands tremble and my knees buckle.

Until this horror came into my life, I felt safe and in control. My life was predictable, my path was mapped out. Now all that's changed.

I think I'd always assumed that pain like this would never come to me. I guess I thought I was immune. But I wasn't. And when it blasted its way into my world, it was like an unexpected punch to the stomach. It took all the wind out of me, and I haven't been able to steady my heart since. I feel so helpless. These events are beyond my control; they seem to be controlling me.

Lord, I seek Your comfort. I seek Your intervention. I need to believe that everything will be okay. I need to feel Your hand of assurance upon me. I need to know that You hear me and that You care. What I really want is to be rescued. Please hear me. Please rescue me from this pain.

Your Distressed Child

A Letter from *Heaven*

Dearest Child,

When you hurt, I hurt too. When you are distressed, I feel your pain.

Even though you are experiencing outward trouble and may feel as if you are wasting away, do not lose heart. For inwardly, I am renewing you day by day.

I will strengthen your feeble hands; I will steady your buckling knees. Be strong and don't fear, for I am your God and I will come and save you. Even if you walk through the valley of death, you do not need to fear, for I am with you. I will guide and protect you as a shepherd does his sheep. I will command My angels to guard you in all your ways. They will hold you in their hands so that you will not be harmed.

Although you are experiencing trouble, I will preserve you. I will stretch out My hand against your foes; with My right hand I will save you. I am your refuge and your strength. I am always by your side when you are having trouble. Even if the whole earth were to give way and the mountains were to fall into the heart of the sea, even then you need not fear. For I am your light and your salvation; I am the fortress of your life. Whom shall you fear with Me here to protect you? For I am close to the brokenhearted, and I save those whose spirits are crushed.

Your God of Rescue

from Isaiah 63:9; 2 Corinthians 4:16–18; Isaiah 35:3–4
Psalms 23:4; 91:11–12; 138:7; 46:1–3; 27:1; 34:18

God's Word OF ENCOURAGEMENT

ISAIAH 63:9

In all their distress he too was distressed, and the angel of his presence saved them. In his love and mercy he redeemed them; he lifted them up and carried them all the days of old.

2 CORINTHIANS 4:16–18

Therefore we do not lose heart. Though outwardly we are wasting away, yet inwardly we are being renewed day by day. For our light and momentary troubles are achieving for us an eternal glory that far outweighs them all. So we fix our eyes not on what is seen, but on what is unseen. For what is seen is temporary, but what is unseen is eternal.

ISAIAH 35:3–4

Strengthen the feeble hands, steady the knees that give way; say to those with fearful hearts, "Be strong, do not fear; your God will come, he will come with vengeance; with divine retribution he will come to save you."

PSALM 27:1

The LORD is my light and my salvation—whom shall I fear? The LORD is the stronghold of my life—of whom shall I be afraid?

PSALM 23:4

Even though I walk through the valley of the shadow of death, I will fear no evil, for you are with me; your rod and your staff, they comfort me.

PSALM 138:7

Though I walk in the midst of trouble, you preserve my life; you stretch out your hand against the anger of my foes, with your right hand you save me.

PSALM 91:11–12

For he will command his angels concerning you to guard you in all your ways; they will lift you up in their hands, so that you will not strike your foot against a stone.

PSALM 46:1–3

God is our refuge and strength, an ever-present help in trouble. Therefore we will not fear, though the earth give way and the mountains fall into the heart of the sea, though its waters roar and foam and the mountains quake with their surging.

PSALM 34:18

The LORD is close to the brokenhearted and saves those who are crushed in spirit.

A LETTER TO *Heaven*

Dear God of Possibilities,

I come before You hoping and praying that You can work a miracle in my heart. There's a lot about me that needs changing. I'm not talking about needing some minor repairs; Lord, I need a complete overhaul. I've tried to change on my own, Lord, but it just hasn't worked. Past mistakes haunt me, and present inadequacies chain me to who I am today—not who I want to become.

I want to experience the personal growth that I know You've called me to, but I don't know how to get started. Failed efforts have discouraged me, and I find it hard to believe that I will ever make any forward progress. I feel powerless to change.

I want the fruit of the Spirit to be in me: love, joy, peace, patience, kindness, goodness, faithfulness, gentleness, and self-control. Those characteristics sound so beautiful but so unlike who I am. I want to live "by the Spirit"; I want to "keep in step with the Spirit," as Your Word says in Galatians 5. But where do I start? How do I begin?

I seek Your help, Lord. I ask that You teach me how to change. I ask that You show me what I need to do to begin the process. I want to be like You.

I eagerly await Your response.

Your Hopeful Child

A Letter from *Heaven*

My Precious Child,

You can have full confidence that I have heard your prayer and that I will act on your behalf. For whenever you pray according to My will—and your desire to be like Me is definitely according to My will—then you can know that you have already received what you have asked of Me.

Your desire for change is the right place to start; now you must put your desire into action so that your willingness is matched by completion. If you desire to be kind, then begin by *doing* something kind. If you desire to be a forgiving person, then begin by *forgiving* someone who has wronged you. If you want to be a loving person, then express your love in *actions*. In order to attain the characteristics you desire, you must pursue them diligently, and you must make every effort to be holy.

Becoming like Me requires that you no longer conform to the ways of this world but that you be transformed by the renewing of your mind. As your mind is changed, you will be able to figure out what My good and perfect will is for your life. As you put your desire into action, you will see Me do amazing things in you, for I am able to do immeasurably more than all you could ask or imagine. My power and My Word are at work in you this very minute.

Your God of Transformation

from 1 John 5:14–15; 2 Corinthians 8:11
Ephesians 4:32; Colossians 3:12; 1 Thessalonians 5:15
2 Timothy 2:24; 1 John 3:18; 1 Timothy 6:11
2 Timothy 2:22; Hebrews 12:14; Romans 12:2
Ephesians 3:20; 1 Thessalonians 2:13

God's Word OF ENCOURAGEMENT

2 CORINTHIANS 8:11
Now finish the work, so that your eager willingness to do it may be matched by your completion of it, according to your means.

EPHESIANS 4:32
Be kind and compassionate to one another, forgiving each other, just as in Christ God forgave you.

COLOSSIANS 3:12
Therefore, as God's chosen people, holy and dearly loved, clothe yourselves with compassion, kindness, humility, gentleness and patience.

HEBREWS 12:14
Make every effort to live in peace with all men and to be holy; without holiness no one will see the Lord.

1 THESSALONIANS 5:15
Make sure that nobody pays back wrong for wrong, but always try to be kind to each other and to everyone else.

1 JOHN 5:15
And if we know that he hears us—whatever we ask—we know that we have what we asked of him.

2 TIMOTHY 2:22

Pursue righteousness, faith, love and peace, along with those who call on the Lord out of a pure heart.

1 THESSALONIANS 2:13

We also thank God continually because, when you received the word of God, which you heard from us, you accepted it not as the word of men, but as it actually is, the word of God, which is at work in you who believe.

ROMANS 12:2

Do not conform any longer to the pattern of this world, but be transformed by the renewing of your mind. Then you will be able to test and approve what God's will is—his good, pleasing and perfect will.

2 TIMOTHY 2:24

The Lord's servant must not quarrel; instead, he must be kind to everyone.

1 TIMOTHY 6:11

Pursue righteousness, godliness, faith, love, endurance and gentleness.

EPHESIANS 3:20

To him who is able to do immeasurably more than all we ask or imagine, according to his power that is at work within us.

A LETTER TO *Heaven*

Dear God,

I desperately need Your help. I don't know how much longer I can resist the tightening grip of defeat on my heart. Every direction I turn, I run up against a brick wall. Every time I try another tactic, that, too, leads to defeat. I'm at a total loss. I don't know which way to go. I've tried so hard. I've done everything I know to do and said everything I know to say. And still—I'm defeated.

If I could have just one small victory, I think I might be able to get up and keep on fighting. But I can't remember any victories. All I remember are countless defeats. I have no more energy. I'm completely drained.

I don't know what to do next, Lord. I've read Your promises of deliverance in the Bible, but I'm at a loss to see it in my life. I come to You with nothing in my hands. I'm begging You, Lord, to step in and offer me some relief. I'm begging You, Lord, to offer me some reason to go on.

Is it worth the effort?

Weary of the Battle

A *Letter* from *Heaven*

Dear Weary Child,

My heart goes out to you, for I am your Father of compassion and your God of all comfort. I know that this life is difficult at times, but be assured that I stand beside you in your battles and that I can guarantee your ultimate victory. In fact, if you will take a firm stand for what is right, you will not have to fight at all; I will do the fighting for you. I promise that at the proper time, you will reap a reward if you do not give up.

I am a mighty God and able to save you. Rest quietly in My love. Listen as I rejoice over you with singing.

You say you have no victory in your life. I have provided you with countless victories! It's just that you've allowed your present distress to overshadow all I've done for you in the past. Remember your earlier days as a believer and how you courageously stood your ground. Don't throw that confidence away! Persevere and do not shrink back, so that in the end you will receive what I have promised.

In reality, I have already given you the victory in Jesus Christ. So do not be afraid, stand firm, and watch My deliverance unfold before your very eyes.

Your God of Victory

from 2 Corinthians 1:3–4; Deuteronomy 20:4
2 Chronicles 20:17; Galatians 6:9; Zephaniah 3:17
Psalm 44:7; Hebrews 10:32, 35–39
1 Corinthians 15:57–58; Exodus 14:13

God's Word OF ENCOURAGEMENT

2 CORINTHIANS 1:3–4
Praise be to the God and Father of our Lord Jesus Christ, the Father of compassion and the God of all comfort, who comforts us in all our troubles.

DEUTERONOMY 20:4
For the LORD your God is the one who goes with you to fight for you against your enemies to give you victory.

1 CORINTHIANS 15:57–58
[God] gives us the victory through our Lord Jesus Christ. Therefore, my dear brothers, stand firm. Let nothing move you.

2 CHRONICLES 20:17
You will not have to fight this battle. Take up your positions; stand firm and see the deliverance the LORD will give you, O Judah and Jerusalem. Do not be afraid; do not be discouraged. Go out to face them tomorrow, and the LORD will be with you.

GALATIANS 6:9
Let us not become weary in doing good, for at the proper time we will reap a harvest if we do not give up.

ZEPHANIAH 3:17
The LORD your God is with you, he is mighty to save. He will take great delight in you, he will quiet you with his love, he will rejoice over you with singing.

EXODUS 14:13
Moses answered the people, "Do not be afraid. Stand firm and you will see the deliverance the LORD will bring you today."

HEBREWS 10:32
Remember those earlier days after you had received the light, when you stood your ground in a great contest in the face of suffering.

PSALM 44:7
You give us victory over our enemies, you put our adversaries to shame.

2 CORINTHIANS 4:8–9
We are hard pressed on every side, but not crushed; perplexed, but not in despair; persecuted, but not abandoned; struck down, but not destroyed.

HEBREWS 10:35–39
So do not throw away your confidence; it will be richly rewarded. You need to persevere so that when you have done the will of God, you will receive what he has promised. For in just a very little while, "He who is coming will come and will not delay. But my righteous one will live by faith. And if he shrinks back, I will not be pleased with him." But we are not of those who shrink back and are destroyed, but of those who believe and are saved.

A LETTER TO *Heaven*

Dearest Father,

I come before You with a growing problem. Every day, the weight of my burden gets bigger and bigger. It's getting to the point where I'm crippled by the guilt I feel over past wrongs. I've hurt so many people, I've lied, I've lived selfishly, and I've made sinful choices—lots of them. And now, Lord, it's all catching up with me.

I've come to know You and Your saving grace in the form of Your Son, Jesus, but for some reason, I have a hard time believing that His grace can really apply to me. I believe that Jesus is Your Son, I've confessed my sins (that took a really long time, and I know I missed many), I have truly repented from my heart, and I was baptized in the name of Your Son. But I still have a hard time accepting that my sins could be so utterly and completely forgiven. To think that my sins could be instantly forgiven because I place my faith and trust in Your Son—it all seems too good to be true.

I want to feel the peace of absolute forgiveness, but I don't know if I dare let down my guard and bask in Your forgiveness for fear that I've not done enough to deserve it.

Please show me the truth of this forgiveness. I long for the peace it could bring. I eagerly await Your reply.

Your Guilt-Ridden Child

A $\mathscr{L}$ETTER FROM *Heaven*

Dear Guilt-Ridden Child,

Don't worry that the process of your forgiveness was too simple. To the contrary, it cost Me the one thing most precious to Me in all the universe—it cost the life of My only Son. From days of old, I have set My heart upon bringing about complete forgiveness to those who trust in Me.

What can you say in response to My great love for you? If I am for you, who can be against you? If I did not spare My own Son, but gave Him up for you, will I not also graciously give you all that you need? Who is there who can bring a charge against you, My chosen one? I am the one who justifies. Who can try to condemn you? Jesus is the one who was raised to life and now sits at My right hand interceding on your behalf.

Though you can never earn the forgiveness that I freely offer you in My Son, I do ask that you live in humble acceptance of what I have given you and that you share this forgiveness with others. You must confess your sins, openly and honestly. You must never claim that you are without sin. You must understand and believe that forgiveness comes only through the shedding of My Son's blood. And you must have a continual attitude of forgiveness toward all others who sin against you.

The peace of forgiveness is already in your possession. Let it freely wash over your soul.

Your God of Forgiveness

from John 3:16; Jeremiah 33:8; 2 Chronicles 7:14
Psalms 65:3; 85:2; Romans 8:31–34; 3:22–24
1 John 1:9, 8, 10; Ephesians 1:7; Hebrews 9:22
Matthew 6:14–15; Luke 6:37

God's Word OF ENCOURAGEMENT

2 CHRONICLES 7:14

If my people, who are called by my name, will humble themselves and pray and seek my face and turn from their wicked ways, then will I hear from heaven and will forgive their sin and will heal their land.

JOHN 3:16

For God so loved the world that he gave his one and only Son, that whoever believes in him shall not perish but have eternal life.

LUKE 6:37

Do not judge, and you will not be judged. Do not condemn, and you will not be condemned. Forgive, and you will be forgiven.

JEREMIAH 33:8

I will cleanse them from all the sin they have committed against me and will forgive all their sins of rebellion against me.

PSALM 65:3

When we were overwhelmed by sins, you forgave our transgressions.

PSALM 85:2

You forgave the iniquity of your people and covered all their sins.

1 JOHN 1:8, 10

If we claim to be without sin, we deceive ourselves and the truth is not in us. If we claim we have not sinned, we make him out to be a liar and his word has no place in our lives.

MATTHEW 6:14–15

If you forgive men when they sin against you, your heavenly Father will also forgive you. But if you do not forgive men their sins, your Father will not forgive your sins.

1 JOHN 1:9

If we confess our sins, he is faithful and just and will forgive us our sins and purify us from all unrighteousness.

ROMANS 3:22–24

This righteousness from God comes through faith in Jesus Christ to all who believe. There is no difference, for all have sinned and fall short of the glory of God, and are justified freely by his grace through the redemption that came by Christ Jesus.

HEBREWS 9:22

In fact, the law requires that nearly everything be cleansed with blood, and without the shedding of blood there is no forgiveness.

EPHESIANS 1:7

In him we have redemption through his blood, the forgiveness of sins, in accordance with the riches of God's grace.

ROMANS 8:31–34

What, then, shall we say in response to this? If God is for us, who can be against us? He who did not spare his own Son, but gave him up for us all-how will he not also, along with him, graciously give us all things? Who will bring any charge against those whom God has chosen? It is God who justifies. Who is he that condemns? Christ Jesus, who died—more than that, who was raised to life—is at the right hand of God and is also interceding for us.

A LETTER TO *Heaven*

Dear Father,

I don't quite know how to say what's on my heart. But if I don't say what's there, I'll never overcome what I'm feeling. The truth is, I'm tired of trying. I'm tired of being nice. I'm tired of being patient. I'm tired of fighting the forces in me that push me away from You. I'm tired of it all.

I'm tempted to just quit! I'm tempted to give in, to give up, to give myself over to the forces I'm resisting.

And yet, Lord, there is a tiny spark in me, a small desire to keep going. The flame is not strong, my will is weak; but, Lord, I do desire to hang on. Instead of giving in to defeat, I want to give myself over to You. But if I am to make it, if I am to keep going, it must be by Your power and Yours alone.

Hold me together, Lord, for I am falling apart. Infuse me with Your strength, for I have none of my own.

Your Weary Child

A *Letter* from *Heaven*

Dearest Child,

You were right to come to Me with your burden, for I am gentle with those who seek My help, and I bring rest to weary souls.

You will find that I do My best work in those who are weak. In fact, My power is made perfect in your weakness. For this reason, you can delight in weakness, in hardship, and in difficulties. When you are at your weakest, then you are truly strong.

In order to tap into My incredible strength, all you must do is come near to Me. When you take just one step toward Me, I will run to meet you with open arms and a loving heart.

I admonish you, My dear child, to take your eyes off of yourself and your burdens and to put them on your big brother, Jesus. Not only did He come to earth and leave all the glory that was His in heaven, but He endured the painful death of the cross and the separation from Me that came with bearing your sin. Think about Him, so that you will not grow weary and lose heart.

I never intended for you to bear the heartaches and burdens of this life alone. My eyes are on you; My ears are attentive to your cry. Do not be dismayed, for I am your God. I will strengthen you and help you; I will uphold you with My righteous right hand.

Your God of Strength

from Matthew 11:28–30; 2 Corinthians 12:9–10
James 4:8; Luke 15:20; Hebrews 12:2–4
Psalm 34:15, 17; Isaiah 41:10

God's Word OF ENCOURAGEMENT

MATTHEW 11:28

Come to me, all you who are weary and burdened, and I will give you rest. Take my yoke upon you and learn from me, for I am gentle and humble in heart, and you will find rest for your souls. For my yoke is easy and my burden is light.

JAMES 4:8

Come near to God and he will come near to you.

LUKE 15:20

While he was still a long way off, his father saw him and was filled with compassion for him; he ran to his son, threw his arms around him and kissed him.

2 CORINTHIANS 12:9–10

He said to me, "My grace is sufficient for you, for my power is made perfect in weakness." Therefore I will boast all the more gladly about my weaknesses, so that Christ's power may rest on me. That is why, for Christ's sake, I delight in weaknesses, in insults, in hardships, in persecutions, in difficulties. For when I am weak, then I am strong.

HEBREWS 12:3–4
Consider him who endured such opposition from sinful men, so that you will not grow weary and lose heart. In your struggle against sin, you have not yet resisted to the point of shedding your blood.

2 THESSALONIANS 3:13
Never tire of doing what is right.

ISAIAH 41:10
So do not fear, for I am with you; do not be dismayed, for I am your God. I will strengthen you and help you; I will uphold you with my righteous right hand.

PSALM 34:15, 17
The eyes of the LORD are on the righteous and his ears are attentive to their cry. The righteous cry out, and the LORD hears them; he delivers them from all their troubles.

A LETTER TO *Heaven*

Dear Father,

I've done it again! I've said something I shouldn't, and I can't unsay it. Sometimes I can hardly believe the things that come out of my mouth. Today I hurt someone I care about very much, at other times I've revealed confidences that were not mine to reveal, and sometimes I say things that are just plain stupid.

Where do these things come from? Sometimes after I've blurted something out, I immediately wish I could pull it right back in. I can't figure out how such words come out of my mouth!

Is there any hope for me? Can I ever learn to control this tongue?

Your Mouthy Child

A LETTER FROM *Heaven*

Dear Child,

The power of the tongue is amazing, isn't it? Its power is like the power of fire: One little spark can set a whole forest ablaze. Words can wound as surely and swiftly as swords and arrows.

But there is hope for you; you can learn to control what comes out of your mouth. Start out by saying less. Remember that I am in heaven and you are on earth, and let your words be few. The more you talk, the greater your chance is of saying something wrong. Wise people know to hold their tongues. Why, even a fool is thought wise if he keeps silent!

As to the origin of the words that come out of your mouth: They come from your heart! So, if you want to clean up your mouth, you must first clean up your heart—for it is out of the overflow of your heart that your mouth speaks.

But there's a positive side to all this too. Your words also have great power for good. One kind word from you can cheer up a friend. A gentle response in a heated discussion can soothe angry feelings. The right word spoken at the right time is as beautiful as golden apples in a silver basket.

Be encouraged, My child, for as My Spirit continues to have His way in you, the results will be love, joy, peace, patience, kindness, goodness, faithfulness, gentleness, and self-control.

Your Loving Father

from James 3:5–6; Psalm 64:3; Ecclesiastes 5:2
Proverbs 10:19; 17:28; Luke 6:45
Proverbs 12:25; 15:1; 25:11; 15:23; Galatians 5:22–23

God's Word OF ENCOURAGEMENT

JAMES 3:5–6
Likewise the tongue is a small part of the body, but it makes great boasts. Consider what a great forest is set on fire by a small spark. The tongue also is a fire, a world of evil among the parts of the body. It corrupts the whole person, sets the whole course of his life on fire, and is itself set on fire by hell.

PSALM 64:3
They sharpen their tongues like swords and aim their words like deadly arrows.

ECCLESIASTES 5:2
Do not be quick with your mouth, do not be hasty in your heart to utter anything before God. God is in heaven and you are on earth, so let your words be few.

PROVERBS 10:19
When words are many, sin is not absent, but he who holds his tongue is wise.

PROVERBS 25:11
A word aptly spoken is like apples of gold in settings of silver.

PROVERBS 12:25
An anxious heart
weighs a man down,
but a kind word
cheers him up.

PROVERBS 17:28
Even a fool is thought wise if he keeps
silent, and discerning if he holds his tongue.

JAMES 4:8
Wash your hands, you sinners,
and purify your hearts, you
double-minded.

PROVERBS 15:23
A man finds joy in giving an apt reply—and
how good is a timely word!

GALATIANS 5:22–23
But the fruit of the Spirit
is love, joy, peace,
patience, kindness, good-
ness, faithfulness, gentleness and self-control.

LUKE 6:45
The good man brings good
things out of the good
stored up in his heart, and
the evil man brings evil
things out of the evil stored
up in his heart. For out of
the overflow of his heart
his mouth speaks.

A LETTER TO *Heaven*

Dearest Father,

It's hard for me to come to You right now because I'm mad and I'm hurt and I'm not sure I want to quit feeling this way just yet. I've had some harsh words with someone I care for, and now one of us is going to have to make the first move to restore our relationship— and I really don't want that someone to be me. But I can't quit thinking of You, and how You always take the first step toward me. That's why I finally came to You. I can't get You off my mind.

I don't even know how we got into the argument—it kind of snuck up on us. And now there's this wall of blame and hurt between us. Open my heart to the possibility that I have contributed to this wall. Let me see the hurt from my loved one's point of view.

You've promised to give me wisdom and insight if I will but seek it, and now I am seeking it, Lord—at least part of me is. Open my eyes to the truth of my responsibility in this breakdown. And then, Lord, give me the courage to face the truth and to focus on what I can do to make things better.

Increase my love, Lord. Take my hand and lead me to the higher road. I'm reaching out, trusting You to take me where I need to be—with my heart opening to Your will.

Needing You

A LETTER FROM *Heaven*

Dearest One,

You have called out to Me, and I have heard you. I always draw near to those who call on Me in truth. And as you begin to see that you, too, had a part in the breakdown of this relationship, you are being truthful.

With your heart open to My leading and shaping, I can grow in you the characteristics that you need. And I've given you the perfect example of the kind of heart you need in order to get along with others—My Son, Jesus! Let your attitude be like His. He had so much concern and love for you and for all your fellow men and women that He gave up all that He had here in heaven with Me—all the glory, all the honor—and He emptied Himself and took on the characteristics of a servant. My Son became a servant!

So you, in being like Him, must lay aside your pride and humble yourself. You must be gentle and patient with your loved one, and you must bear with your friend in love. I want you to go so far as to consider the interests of this person who's hurt you more than you consider your own. While this may not be easy, you can do it through My strength and the strength of My Son.

Put your love into action by following the example of My Son; then trust in Me to work in you. Together, we can work it out.

Your Loving Father

from Psalm 145:18; Philippians 1:6; 2:5–7
Ephesians 4:2l; Philippians 2:3–4; 4:13

God's Word OF ENCOURAGEMENT

PSALM 145:18
The LORD is near to all who call on him, to all who call on him in truth.

EPHESIANS 4:2
Be completely humble and gentle; be patient, bearing with one another in love.

PHILIPPIANS 4:13
I can do everything through him who gives me strength.

PHILIPPIANS 1:6
He who began a good work in you will carry it on to completion until the day of Christ Jesus.

PHILIPPIANS 2:3–4
Do nothing out of selfish ambition or vain conceit, but in humility consider others better than yourselves. Each of you should look not only to your own interests, but also to the interests of others.

PHILIPPIANS 2:5–7
Your attitude should be the same as that of Christ Jesus: Who, being in very nature God, did not consider equality with God something to be grasped, but made himself nothing, taking the very nature of a servant, being made in human likeness.

A Letter to *Heaven*

Dear Father,

What a gracious, loving God You are! I praise You for Your infinite love, for Your ever-present care, for Your abundant blessings.

Today my heart is overflowing with Your joy—a joy that springs from deep inside of me, a joy that is founded in You. So often I come to You burdened with pain or asking You for help. And I know that You are more than happy to hear me—no matter why I come to You—but today, I come to celebrate Your deep, abiding joy that remains with me even in the darkest times.

As I look at my life, I see Your blessings at every turn. Though I've had my share of difficulties, when I look back at them, I see that You were always with me—right in the middle of my pain. Your light is constantly shining, even in the blackest night. And I've observed a comforting truth as You've walked with me day by day—I've learned that it is Your strength that fills me with joy. When I feel weak and inadequate, I turn to You for help, and as You supply me with Your strength, a deep sense of joy fills my soul and I am once again calmed by Your peace.

Thank You for creating in me a joy that is not defined by "happiness." I can be in the most unhappy circumstances, yet I am confident and comforted by Your ever-present joy. Along with all of creation, I praise You for Your abiding presence.

Your Joyful Child

A *LETTER FROM Heaven*

Dear Joyful Child,

How pleased I am that you are learning the true meaning and source of joy. As you take My Word into your heart, My teachings will be a constant source of joy to you, and your eyes will sparkle with My light. If you obey My commands, you will remain in My love, and your joy will be complete.

And as My joy grows in your heart, you will grow in your understanding that My strength and My joy are constant companions. My joy stored up in your heart will make you strong, for My joy is your strength. Your heart will leap for joy as you trust in Me and lean on My strength. You can be confident that my light shines even in your darkest troubles and that even the night will shine like the day, for darkness is like light to Me.

Just look around at the creation, and you will see that all of nature joins you in your joy. The rivers clap their hands, and the mountains sing together. The fields are jubilant, and the trees of the forest sing for joy. When I comfort you, the heavens shout for joy and the earth rejoices. Because I have forgiven your sins and swept away your offenses like a cloud, the mountains burst into song.

Because you live your life for Me, you can rest assured that all your tomorrows carry the promise of My deep, abiding joy.

Your God of Everlasting Joy

from Psalm 19:8; John 15:10–11; Nehemiah 8:10 Psalms 28:7; 18:28; 139:11–12; 98:8; 96:12; Isaiah 49:13; 44:22-23; Proverbs 10:28

God's Word OF ENCOURAGEMENT

PSALM 18:28
You, O LORD, keep my lamp burning; my God turns my darkness into light.

PSALM 126:5–6
Those who sow in tears will reap with songs of joy. He who goes out weeping, carrying seed to sow, will return with songs of joy, carrying sheaves with him.

PSALM 19:8
The precepts of the LORD are right, giving joy to the heart. The commands of the LORD are radiant, giving light to the eyes.

PROVERBS 10:28
The prospect of the righteous is joy.

ISAIAH 49:13
Shout for joy, O heavens; rejoice, O earth; burst into song, O mountains! For the LORD comforts his people and will have compassion on his afflicted ones.

PSALM 139:11–12
If I say, "Surely the darkness will hide me and the light become night around me," even the darkness will not be dark to you; the night will shine like the day, for darkness is as light to you.

NEHEMIAH 8:10

The joy of the LORD is your strength.

JOHN 15:10–11

If you obey my commands, you will remain in my love, just as I have obeyed my Father's commands and remain in his love. I have told you this so that my joy may be in you and that your joy may be complete.

PSALM 98:8

Let the rivers clap their hands, let the mountains sing together for joy,

ISAIAH 44:22–23

"I have swept away your offenses like a cloud, your sins like the morning mist. Return to me, for I have redeemed you." Sing for joy, O heavens, for the LORD has done this; shout aloud, O earth beneath. Burst into song, you mountains, you forests and all your trees, for the LORD has redeemed Jacob, he displays his glory in Israel.

PSALM 96:12

Let the fields be jubilant, and everything in them. Then all the trees of the forest will sing for joy.

PSALM 28:7

The LORD is my strength and my shield; my heart trusts in him, and I am helped. My heart leaps for joy and I will give thanks to him in song.

Other great gift books from Howard Publishing:

Heavenly Mail Series:
Heavenly Mail: Words of Promise from God

Hugs Series:
Hugs for Friends
Hugs for Dad
Hugs for Kids
Hugs for Mom
Hugs for Sisters
Hugs for Women
Hugs for Teachers
Hugs for Those in Love
Hugs for Grandparents
Hugs for the Holidays
Hugs for the Hurting
Hugs to Encourage and Inspire
Hugs for Grads
Hugs for Grandma

Hugs from Heaven Series:
Hugs from Heaven: Embraced by the Savior
Hugs from Heaven: On Angel Wings
Hugs from Heaven: The Christmas Story
Hugs from Heaven: Celebrating Friendship
Hugs from Heaven: Portraits of a Woman's Faith

Heartlifters Series:
Heartlifters for Mom
Heartlifters for Friends
Heartlifters for Women
Heartlifters for Hope and Joy
Heartlifters for Teachers
Heartlifters for the Young at Heart